RUSSIA

Building Democracy

John Bradley

In post-communist Russia, food queues still exist, despite economic reforms.

A WATTS BOOK

LONDON • SYDNEY • LONDON • SYDNEY • LONDON • SYDNEY • LONDON • SYDNEY

Yeltsin gets a Welcome Vote of Confidence

1993 election triumph

The 1993 elections increased Boris Yeltsin's power as President.

IN 1993 the first free elections in post-Soviet Russia were hailed as a triumph for democracy over communism, the political system introduced by the Communist Party to the former Soviet Union (USSR).

But democracy has not brought an instant solution to Russia's problems. Inflation caused prices to rise by 1,300 per cent in 1993. Many people have lost their jobs. Until 1991 the economy was run by the state. Private business is now taking over, and this has led to a fall in Russia's wealth.

Although Boris Yeltsin was endorsed as President in the elections, he disagrees with the Prime Minister, Victor Chernomyrdin, on how to continue reforming Russia. As a result of these elections, the parliament is dominated by extreme nationalists and former communists, who dislike change.

Monde

re, 75501 Paris Cedex 15

FONDATEUR : HUBE

rlift fias

n Says

Water Rwandans trek

ite 'H

Ν ΠΟΛΙΤΙΚΗ ΗΓΕΣ

constitución...
réndum será una prueba
Moldavia ha elegi
mocracia

ne police went in afte
Jemonstrators pelted them with
bottles, cans and sticks.
The violence erupted during
narch organised by the Socia
Workers' Party in protest at
minal Justice Bill.

the iron
ing Street a m
and tried to
Only a lock a
chain kept th
A squad of
gear charge
times befor
quelled.
Police w
long-handl
time durin
went on f
Twelve
arrested

ΥΛΩΝsses targets JUNGL

can peo
is as an excu

DAILY MIRROR, Tuesday, March

ΩΠΗΣ CSA PAY DUNGL
LEFT ME BRO!

αι αρχηγοί κομμάτων
ε τον Κληρίδη εκτάκτω

EXCLUSIVE
By ROGER TODD

My bank manager can't
see any option as I haven't
any money left to live on.
"I appealed against the
CSA assessment
summer but they
no notice. Th
forced my em
hand it all over
"I can't be
dictatorial
agency behav

ερικές προδήλως αρνητικές για την Κύ
Συμβούλιο της Ευρώπης, συμμεριζετα
ς Κληρίδης, που: Σύντομα θα θέσει προσ
αση, προκειμένου να δρομολογηθούν απ
τόχο την αποτροπή χωριστής εκπροσώπ
σης των Τ/Κυπρίων.

A DIVORCED father
has wrongly had £634
a month docked from
his pay by the Child
Support Agency.
The outrageous bungle
has forced crane driver
Roy Sullivan to:
PUT his £40,000 house up
for sale.
SELL his Ford Escort
ar, and
HAVE his phone cut off
Desperate 36-year-old
is now off work
from a stomach
stress.
the CSA
puter for

agency fixed Roy's main-
tenance deductions at
£1,004 a month.
Then it found he was
being charged not only for
his two daughters - but for
a child who isn't his.
The agency apologised
and reduced the deduction
order attached to his
earnings.
But Roy, from Cardiff,
still hasn't had a refund.
He said: "I earn £300 a
week but after deductions
I didn't have enough left
to pay my £300 mortgage.
"I've had the 'For Sale'
n up for several weeks
rests of justice over
the PIIC does no
my view."
has stated

Appa

Labour
Jones, w
Roy'
appalli
"Th
bank
big
m
al

Κι αυτό προκύπτει από χθε
νη συνάντηση του Προεδρο,
με τον πρόεδρο της Βουλή
Αλέξη Γαλανό, που τον ενημ
νω σε κάποιες λεπτομε
προαγονται στ
το

新交 相互

MUNDO

DEL SIGLO VEINTIUNO

No desesperéis jamás; y si desesperáis seguid trabajando. (Burke)

A» EN EL DIA INTERNACIONAL DE

mag
who helpeu
itors that
and

© Aladdin Books Ltd 1995

Designed and produced by
Aladdin Books Ltd
28 Percy Street
London W1P OLD

First published in
Great Britain in 1995 by
Watts Books
96 Leonard Street
London EC2A 4RH

Editor: Katie Roden
Designer: Tessa Barwick
Illustrator: David Burroughs
Picture research: Brooks Krikler Research

The author, **John Bradley**, has taught Russian and Eastern European
history and politics for over 30 years. He lectured at the Universities of
Manchester, Southern California and Maryland. He is also the author
of numerous books on Eastern Europe and international affairs.
The consultant, **Dr John Channon**, is Senior Lecturer at the School of
Slavonic and Eastern European Studies, University of London.
He researches and writes on historical and contemporary
developments in Russia.

Printed in Belgium

A CIP catalogue record for this book is available from the
British Library

ISBN: 0 7496 2179 6

The 'Near Abroad'

MANY of the former Soviet republics (the 'near abroad') contain many Russians as well as other ethnic groups. This mixture is a potential source of conflict. The newly independent states still rely on their pre-1991 economic links with Russia.

The old Soviet Union (right) had many peoples and states who were keen to get independence. The new Russian Federation (below) contains 16 non-Russian, self-governing republics, such as Bashkirostan and Chechenya (see page 26).

SOVIET UNION (USSR)

Arctic Ocean

MONGOLIA

IRAN

CHINA

BRITAIN

DENMARK

NORWAY

SWEDEN

LITHUANIA

LATVIA

ESTONIA

FINLAND

POLAND

BELARUS

UKRAINE

MOLDOVA

Black Sea

TURKEY

GEORGIA

ARMENIA

IRAQ

AZERBAIJAN

IRAN

Caspian Sea

TURKMENISTAN

UZBEKISTAN

Aral Sea

KAZAKHSTAN

THE RUSSIAN FEDERATION

Arctic Ocean

Barents Sea

Kara Sea

Laptev Sea

Bering Sea

Sea of Okhotsk

MONGOLIA

CHINA

AFGHANISTAN

TAJIKISTAN

KYRGYZSTAN

JAPAN

NORTH KOREA

SOUTH KOREA

An Ailing Economy

Democracy brings hardship

Fast food arrives in Moscow: Yeltsin visits a McDonalds, 1993.

RUSSIA is no longer a superpower, as it was under communism, and it needs financial aid to rebuild its economy. Although it is still a military giant, Russia's political and economic standing has been steadily decreasing since the break-up of the Soviet Union in 1991.

The USA believes that helping Russia is the cheapest way to ensure world stability. But it fears that if the extreme nationalist Vladimir Zhirinovsky (see page 25) became President, he would use Russia's nuclear weapons to threaten the world.

Russia keeps military forces in the former Soviet republics, to prevent civil wars and keep their governments in power. It also protects Slavs outside its borders, and unsuccessfully tried to help the peace in Bosnia.

The Triumph of Russian Nationalism

The parliament (State Duma) contains 152 Reformers (Yeltsin's supporters), 197 Anti-Reformers and 101 independents. It is dominated by nationalist Anti-Reformers, who aim to give Russia power over the rest of the world and to ensure that Russians have rights over non-Russians within the country. The Duma could therefore block Yeltsin's reforms, so he chooses to rule by issuing decrees (laws which come into force immediately) rather than by discussion.

Fruit and vegetables are too expensive for most Russians.

Ethnic Tensions Remain

Racial issues are important both within and outside the Russian Federation.

RUSSIANS make up about 83 per cent of the population, but within the country there are areas dominated by peoples such as Tatars, Ukrainians, Chuvash, Bashkirs, Belarusians, Mordvins, Chechens, Udmurts, Mari, Kazakhs, Avars, Jews and Armenians.

The nationalist Vladimir Zhirinovksy wants to break with Russia's neighbours. This has forced the neighbouring countries to strengthen their relations with Russia. Armenia has accepted Russian troops on its soil in return for oil and wheat, which it badly needs.

Russian troops in Azerbaijan have helped to prevent a civil war and have intervened in fighting in Moldova. About 25,000 Russian troops are in Tajikistan to protect it against Afghan raids. Georgia has asked for Russian help in dealing with Abkhaz separatists.

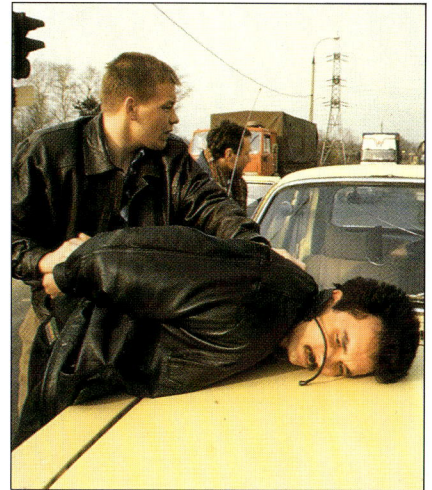

Crime is growing: the police are trying to deal with a huge increase in gangs since 1990.

Free Market Stimulates Mafia Power

Under communism, Mafias (powerful criminal groups) were kept under control by the threat of severe punishments. Many Moscow criminals belonged to the Georgian Mafia, which ran fruit and vegetable supplies. After the break-up of the USSR in 1991, the military Mafia developed, selling cheap weapons to former enemies. This caused disputes between several Mafia gangs, and led to some murders. The Chechen Mafia specialised in timber exports and drug smuggling, and fought bitter battles in Europe and the USA. It is widely thought that the Italian Mafia used Russian Mafias to smuggle drugs from Russia into the USA.

Armenian carpet traders still sell their wares in Russia.

Huge price rises have forced many poor Russians to scavenge for their food on rubbish tips.

National and Social Upheavals

SINCE THE collapse of the USSR, the road to democracy has not been easy. An initial monthly inflation rate of 20-50 per cent pushed prices up. Industrial output has fallen and, according to official figures, 6 per cent of the workforce are unemployed.

Russia's fragile democracy faces two enemies: the shock to the people caused by the recent political upheavals, and economic chaos.

Bashkirostan and Chechenya are now trying to break away from Russian control. Troops are returning from abroad, to face possible unemployment.

Violent crime is increasing dramatically, and several important public figures have been murdered. In 1992, 2.7 million crimes were committed in Russia – a 27 per cent increase on 1991. However, the country does not have enough money to cover the costs of fighting organised crime, which is growing fast.

Rebuilding the Economy

Radical reforms are being introduced

RUSSIA'S ECONOMY has been in chaos for many years. The Reformers want to take industry and agriculture out of state control and put them into private hands.

By 1994, 20,000 businesses were privately owned, and nearly 60 per cent of Russia's national wealth was provided by the newly created private sector. The remaining state-owned businesses are being sold for cash. However, this rapid change has caused its own problems. Thousands of private businesses are nearly bankrupt, and private enterprises owe the government 30 trillion roubles (£3.8 billion) in unpaid debts.

Many factories have old-fashioned equipment.

On the positive side, the government has brought the annual inflation rate down, from 1,300 per cent in 1993 to 202 per cent in 1994.

Harming the Environment

Industrial waste from timber factories has polluted Lake Baikal.

UNDER communism, pollution was a major problem. The drive to improve industrial production meant that the environment suffered. Toxic waste was pumped directly into the earth. Air pollution from inefficient factories has led to health problems. Both the Caspian and the Aral Seas are shrinking, because water has been diverted from them for use in irrigation projects.

In October 1994 a badly maintained oil pipeline in Siberia broke, and up to 321 million litres of oil were spilt.

Traditional farming methods are still used in many areas.

Years Behind the West

Russian industry and agriculture are very outdated, and there are few public services.

UNDER COMMUNISM, much investment, research and development went into nuclear weapons and military vehicles, to strengthen the Soviet Union's position as a world superpower.

However, agriculture was badly run and there was much waste. Industrial equipment was old fashioned, while consumer goods and cars were badly copied from Western models. Workers were poorly paid and their output was low.

Managers were often sacked if they did not achieve certain targets, so many faked their production statistics. Because of this, Russia is now 20 years behind other industrialised countries in modern technology, especially in computers.

The Nuclear Industry

After the Second World War (1939-45), the Soviet government concentrated on the development of nuclear weapons. Research institutes were established, using all the scientific resources available, and scientific teams kept up the nuclear 'arms race' with the USA until the 1980s. For a short while the USSR led the world in missile development. Nuclear submarines and nuclear-powered ships became the pride of communism. Space exploration and nuclear energy development also increased. Safety was often a low priority, and there were many accidents. The disposal of nuclear waste was inefficient: in 1994, at one disposal site, waste began to spread uncontrollably.

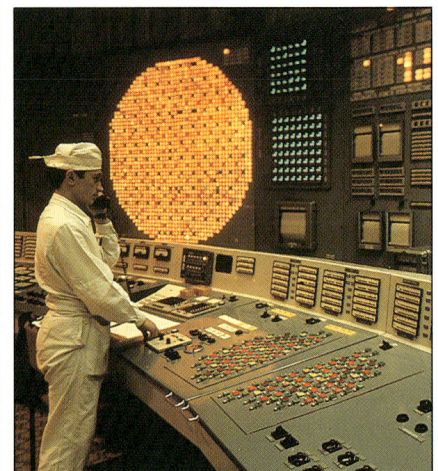

Safety may be poor in nuclear power stations and factories.

BORIS YELTSIN:

"In August 1991, over night, a new Russia – 'Boris Yeltsin's Russia' – took the place of the Soviet Union."

Mother Russia

WHAT WE today call southern Russia used to be ruled by nomadic peoples, and the north by Finns and Lithuanians. Vikings probably invaded the area and called it 'Rus'. In the ninth century AD, Slavic peoples set up a state around Kiev. They held meetings to debate policies, which were carried out by elders.

Vladimir I (c. 978-1015) seized the throne of Kiev for himself after defeating his brothers. He converted to Christianity in 987, and so did many of the Slavic peoples. This was an important step towards the inclusion of Russia into Christian Europe. Vladimir was later made a saint in memory of this conversion. He founded the Russian Orthodox Church, which is still popular today.

Vladimir's I's icon is believed to protect against all sorts of evils.

The Rise of Nationalism

In 1206 *Gengis Khan* assumed leadership of the Mongol tribes, whom he led in the conquest of China and Central Asia. This also included southern Russia, whose armies were defeated at Kalka in 1228. This far-reaching conquest and rule of lands was known as the 'Tatar Yoke'.

*An icon by the famous religious painter **Andrei Rublev** (c. 1360-1430).*

IN THE EARLY thirteenth century, Mongolian peoples, fighting a mobile warfare on horseback, swept through the Central Asian plains and the southeast of Russia. Led by Gengis Khan, the Mongols, called Tatars by the Russians, conquered huge amounts of land.

In 1237 Gengis' grandson, Batu Khan, invaded Russia once again. In 1240 he destroyed the city of Kiev because its elders refused to pay tribute to him.

The Tatars devastated Galicia, Hungary, Poland and Silesia, then disappeared suddenly into the depths of Asia. They left behind a trail of destruction.

The army of Novgorod, which survived the Mongol invasion.

This map shows the expansion of the Russian empire (1360-1917), from its initial beginnings in the present capital, Moscow, until the year of the revolution in 1917.

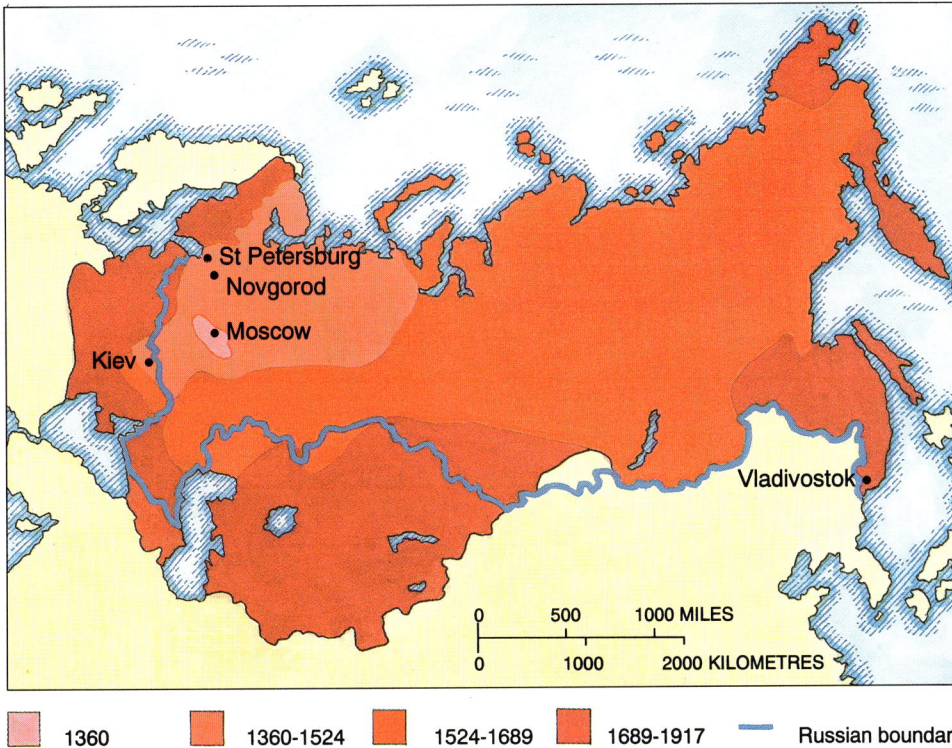

1360	1360-1524	1524-1689	1689-1917		Russian boundary

Ivan IV (ruled 1556-84), known as 'the Terrible', became Tsar (emperor) of 'all Russia'. He was called 'Terrible' because he created a state by ruthless means. He used his secret police to kill rebellious nobles, and took their lands.

Peter the Great (Peter I, 1682-1725) decided to transform Russia into a modern empire ruled by himself rather than by elders. He formed a nobility to lead the , and a secret police to carry out his policies.

The Tatars demanded heavy tribute from the cities they took. After the Tatar invasions, the traders of Novgorod and the princes of Moscow prospered. In 1380 the Great Prince of Moscow, Dmitry Donskoy, defeated a Tatar chieftain at Kulikovo, but two years later Moscow was overthrown.

At the end of the fourteenth century, the Tatars were defeated by another Asian chief, Tamerlane. In 1450 they divided into three 'Hordes': Kazan, Astrakhan and Crimean. Basil II (1425-62) further expanded Moscow's lands, and Ivan III (1462-1505) claimed Novgorod and other princedoms. In 1480 he ended the Tatars' power, and declared his independence.

Basil III tore the country apart by fighting the Orthodox Church.

In 1556 Ivan IV ('the Terrible') became Tsar of Russia, defeated the Kazan Horde, and expanded eastward. His attempts to expand westward were not so successful: in 1570 he destroyed Novgorod when it rose against him. Ivan was succeeded by his son Theodore in 1584, who died heirless in 1598. This led to a 'Time of Troubles' (1605-13), when many ineffectual people claimed the throne.

By the time Peter the Great became emperor in 1682, Russia included the whole of Siberia. He improved the Russian army, beat the last Tatars and moved the capital to his new city, St Petersburg.

Tradition versus Reform

AFTER SOME ineffectual successors to Peter I, Catherine II ('the Great') tried to increase Russian wealth. She won land in Poland, but was almost overthrown by a rebellion in 1773. After Catherine came several emperors with conflicting policies. Some wanted reform; others were against it.

Catherine the Great (ruled 1762-96) became Empress by having her husband strangled. She encouraged Russian literature and culture.

Alexander I (ruled 1801-25) won the Napoleonic Wars against France in 1812.

The Napoleonic Wars made Alexander I into a great Russian hero.

Under Alexander I, Russia became involved in the historic Napoleonic Wars, and Moscow was occupied by the French army until 1812. However, in October of that year the Russian army drove the French out, and later entered France itself. As he rode triumphantly into Paris, Alexander became a great hero of the Russian people.

Alexander II (ruled 1855-81) freed the peasants from serfdom, but was assassinated in 1881 by a group of revolutionaries called People's Will.

But he quickly lost their respect, with a series of thoughtless and oppressive changes.

Nicholas I (ruled 1825-55) re-established the secret police. He imprisoned his opponents in mental hospitals or sent them to Siberia, the wastelands in the east of Russia. He became involved in a disastrous war against England and France in the Crimea.

His son, Alexander II (ruled 1855-81), signed a peace treaty with England and France. Alexander also launched a series of reforms to lift Russia out of its economic decline. In 1861 Russian peasants were freed from serfdom to their masters.

Yet many peasants had duties to their villages and could not go to work in the rapidly developing cities. The freeing of the peasants was never finished and there was much unrest, including terrorist attacks. In 1880 the secret police was re-established, but Alexander was assassinated by a revolutionary organisation in 1881.

Alexander III (ruled 1881-94) kept Russia under military law, but he could not stamp out terrorism. Despite this, he introduced many economic and social improvements, and Russian armies conquered nearby countries such as parts of China, Korea, Central Asia and Turkey's Balkan lands.

Feodor Dostoevsky (1821-81) was a novelist. He joined a group of socialists who discussed banned books. In 1849 they were sentenced to death, but Dostoevsky's sentence was reduced to hard labour in Siberia.

*Peter Tchaikovsky (1840-93) was a musician whose music, especially his compositions for ballets such as **Swan Lake**, enchanted the world. He was part of a 'golden age' of Russian music, with many other composers.*

The Rise of the Soviet Union

Nicholas II switched between reform and police rule. However, Russia caught up with Western Europe in several areas of its economic development.

Grigory Rasputin (1872-1916), a religious teacher, claimed to have powers which kept Nicholas' ill son alive. He was powerful at court, but he was assassinated in 1916.

NICHOLAS II (ruled 1894-1917) tried to keep Russia as his father Alexander III had left it. However, in 1905 Russia was defeated in an unpopular war against Japan. In the same year Nicholas' troops opened fire on a peaceful demonstration of workers, and the Russian people rose up in the country's first revolution, against the military government.

Nicholas promised elections and a committee (Duma) with which he would share power. But he did not keep his promises. His Prime Minister, Peter Stolypin, failed to complete the reforms and was assassinated in 1911. Russia was placed under police rule again.

Despite this, Russia's industrial development was amazing. It was a major producer of iron, steel, textiles, minerals, oil and alcohol. Life began to improve, as housing and education developed. But the First World War (1914-18) put an end to this progress.

Fires raged over Moscow during the people's revolution of 1905.

In 1914 Austria-Hungary and Germany began a war with France, Britain and Russia (the Western Allies). The war lasted four years and by 1917 Russia was in a state of collapse. In March 1917 Nicholas was overthrown after a revolution of the people.

A new Provisional Government was formed. In October the Russian Bolshevik party, led by Vladimir Lenin, started another revolution. Between 1918 and 1920 the Bolsheviks, known as the Reds, fought their opponents, known as the Whites, in a bloody civil war.

Lenin inspired the Moscow crowds during the 1917 revolution.

The Bolsheviks won, and began to govern through communism – the political system which believes society should be classless and land, factories and other property should be owned by everyone rather than by individuals.

Russia, now called the Russian Soviet Federative Socialist Republic (RSFSR), was in ruins after the civil war and was isolated from anti-communist countries. In 1922 it was re-named the Union of Soviet Socialist Republics (USSR), when the RSFSR joined with several other republics.

Lenin died in 1924 and was succeeded by Josef Stalin, who put many of the aims of communism into practice. Collectivisation was introduced, in which farmers and peasants were forced to give their lands to the state. Industry was controlled from Moscow by a group of economic planners. Stalin used terror to force these changes through. There were severe punishments, including death, for people who would not give up their lands. Stalin even killed many of his allies because they disagreed with his policies.

Lenin (real name Vladimir Illych Ulyanov, 1870-1924) was the Bolshevik leader of the revolution in October 1917. He introduced communism to Russia, wanting to create social justice and wealth in the country.

Trotsky (real name Lev Davidovich Bronstein, 1879-1940) led the Bolshevik military forces. He fell out with Stalin, who exiled him to Central Asia in 1928 and had him assassinated in 1940.

The **Great Patriotic War**

Andrei Vyshinsky (1883-1954) was Stalin's hangman in the purges of 1933-37. During the Second World War he was a diplomat for Stalin, then became his foreign minister.

The cavalry of the Red Army rode small, agile horses which moved quickly over the snowy landscape and could cover over 100 km (60 miles) in a night.

Civilians endured great hardships during the Patriotic War.

IN AUGUST 1939 Stalin and the German Nazi leader, Adolf Hitler, signed an agreement not to attack each other. Within days, Hitler's troops invaded Poland and started the Second World War (1939-45).

Stalin and Hitler planned to divide the world between them. In 1940 Hitler defeated France, and Stalin annexed the Baltic republics.

Yet the alliance between Hitler and Stalin was unstable, as the leaders had different interests. In the summer of 1941, after the conquest of nearly all of Europe, Hitler invaded the USSR and the Great Patriotic War began.

By now Stalin's armies were weak, and they collapsed before the Nazis. The German army reached Leningrad and conquered Ukraine but were stopped at the gates of Moscow. Stalin had called for fresh troops from Siberia, who halted the German advance in the terrible winter of 1941. Hitler advanced southward in 1942, but was defeated in Stalingrad.

Hitler's armies were slowly driven out of the western parts of the USSR. In early 1945 the Soviet army reached the eastern parts of Germany, Romania, Hungary, Yugoslavia and Bulgaria. Later that year, at Yalta, Stalin met the Allied leaders Franklin D. Roosevelt of the USA and Winston Churchill of Britain. They divided the world into zones and agreed to form the United Nations (UN), a peacekeeping organisation.

While the Western Allies defeated the Nazi armies in the west and south of Germany, Soviet troops advanced through Austria and Czechoslovakia to reach Hitler's capital, Berlin. On 30 April 1945 Hitler committed suicide, and on 8 May Germany surrendered. The Soviet Union and communism had survived the Nazi destruction, but at a terrible cost to the people of about 40 million lives.

The Soviet Red Army took the German capital, Berlin, in 1945.

JOSEF STALIN (real name Iosif Vissarionovich Dzhugashvili, 1879-1953) was born in Georgia in a shoemaker's family. He started to train as an orthodox priest, but was exiled to Siberia for revolutionary activity. In 1917 he took part in the Bolshevik rising, then in the civil war. He succeeded Lenin in 1924, and murdered his rivals in the 1930s. His policy of forced collectivisation caused many millions of deaths between 1928 and 1939 – a time called the 'Great Terror' – due to poverty and oppressive laws. During the Second World War, while Russia was allied to Britain and the USA, battles against the German army cost the Soviet Union more than 20 million soldiers. A similar number of civilians probably died at the same time.

The Cold War

The superpowers compete for world domination

IN JULY-AUGUST 1945 the Allies met to start the process of peacemaking, but they began to quarrel. Roosevelt had ended the war with Japan by dropping two atom bombs, and no longer needed the USSR as an ally. Stalin also had an atom bomb, and wanted to spread communism worldwide.

Stalin met the Western leaders for the last time as an ally at Potsdam, Germany, in 1945.

Nikita Khrushchev (1894-1972), Stalin's eventual successor, denounced Stalin in 1956 but changed little in the Stalinist system of government. Under his rule, more consumer goods were produced. In 1964 he was dismissed as leader after mistakes which almost brought him into conflict with the USA.

Leonid Brezhnev (1906-82) was a plotter against Khrushchev, who eventually became his successor. He tried to make peace with the USA, but he never stuck to agreements. After 1975, the USSR became involved in overseas wars and fell into an economic crisis, which the ageing leader could not resolve.

Soon the former Allies were arguing over Berlin, Czechoslovakia, Yugoslavia and Austria. They then fought each other in 1950 in Korea. This 'cold war' continued until the death of Stalin in 1953.

After his death, the cold war seemed to simmer down for a time. The two sides signed a peace agreement in Korea, but the country remained divided between communists in the north and non-communists in the south. The Soviet Union returned to the United Nations, where a series of meetings tried to solve the problems of the cold war.

However, the world powers were still divided, between NATO (the North Atlantic Treaty Organisation representing the Western countries) and the Warsaw Pact (representing the Soviet Union and its allies).

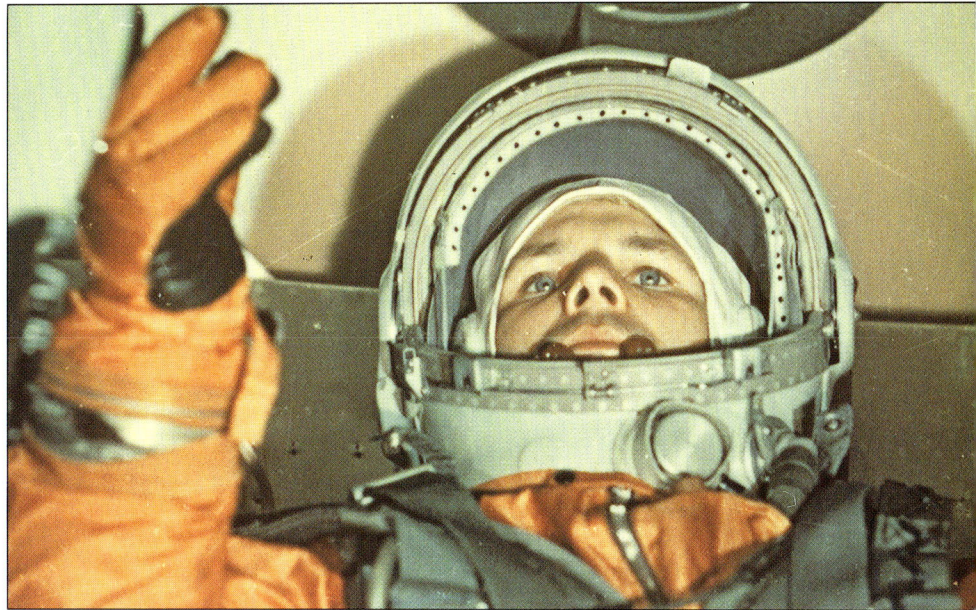

Major Yuri Gagarin was the first person in space in 1961. The Soviet Union competed with the USA in the 'space race'.

In 1956 there was a strong uprising against communism in Hungary, which was crushed by Soviet tanks. After that the cold war became more intense, with clashes between East and West in Berlin, Vietnam and South America.

In 1962 the USSR threatened to establish nuclear missile bases on Cuba, but this was opposed by the USA. The crisis frightened both sides into trying to avoid the threat of nuclear war. They began to talk, but without success.

Yuri Andropov (1913-84) began his career in the KGB, or secret police. He was a tough leader, who persecuted those who disagreed with him. He was chosen as a successor to Brezhnev because he hated corruption, which he saw as the cause of the economic crisis. However, he died before he could achieve any real reforms.

Konstantin Chernenko (1912-85) was the general secretary of the Communist Party who succeeded Yuri Andropov in 1984, only to die within months. He was aged 73 and in poor health at the time of his appointment. During his period in office, he handed most of his power to his eventual successor, Mikhail Gorbachev.

"Lots of smoke was billowing out of the damaged reactor...and injured firemen were being carried out. I didn't think about safety, none of us did..."

The Soviet Empire

*Alexander Solzhenitsyn is a writer whose book **Gulag Archipelago** exposed Stalin's reign of terror. He was exiled and settled in the USA.*

Andrei Sakharov, a physicist, criticised Soviet nuclear development. He was exiled, but returned to Moscow in 1986.

IN 1968 the Soviet army invaded Czechoslovakia, when the country's government tried to reform communism. By 1972 the USSR and USA had signed arms control treaties. After the USA lost the Vietnam War in 1975, they at last tried to talk about disarming.

Czech people unsuccessfully tried to resist Soviet tanks in 1968.

However, the Soviet leader Leonid Brezhnev failed to stick to any agreements. By the 1980s the US President Ronald Reagan had named the USSR the 'evil empire'.

In the early 1980s the Soviet Union faced an economic crisis. It could only feed its population by importing grain from Western countries and its industry, apart from the weapons industry, had fallen apart. It could not afford its huge military capacity, and its people had no personal freedom.

"We must re-structure our economy ... identify faults through glasnost and democratise our lives to become really free."

The wreckage of Chernobyl.

Soviet troops were occupying Czechoslovakia, and after 1979 the USSR was involved in a war in Afghanistan. It was threatened by NATO missiles in Western Europe, had roles in African wars, and had to sort out potential conflicts in Asia. It was overstretched and in danger of collapse.

Mikhail Gorbachev became President in 1985. He launched a campaign called perestroika (reconstruction). New people would control the economy, and there would be new systems for running industry.

Many people opposed these changes, so Gorbachev tried another method, called glasnost (openness). This would allow him to detect ministers opposed to perestroika. But to achieve this he had to end the cold war with the USA.

Gorbachev and Reagan agreed to disarm in 1985. But the USSR was still criticised for its lack of freedom, especially after an accident at the Chernobyl nuclear plant in 1986, when the local people were not warned about radioactivity. Gorbachev needed the West's help, so had to democratise the USSR.

A poster for perestroika.

ПРИСТРОЙКА К ПЕРЕСТРОЙКЕ

MIKHAIL GOR-BACHEV became leader of the Communist Party in 1985. He differed from other leaders in being relatively young. He was born in 1931 in Stavropol, an agricultural region in the southeast of the USSR. In 1978 he was called to Moscow to supervise agriculture. He travelled abroad, seeing how other countries produced food. In Canada he met A. Yakovlev, an exiled party official, who agreed with his ideas on rebuilding the economy. He later found another ally in Edward Shevardnadze, a member of the communist leadership. Eventually, this trio introduced perestroika, glasnost and demokratizat-siya (democratisation).

DANIEL YERGIN, 1995:

"Everything Russians took for granted – economic security, queues...safety...the KGB...the Soviet Union as a superpower – it's all gone."

The Collapse of the USSR

Perestroika in trouble: queues lengthen and the shops are empty

In 1989 new-style Soviet elections took place. Among those elected was Boris Yeltsin, the future President of the Russian Federation.

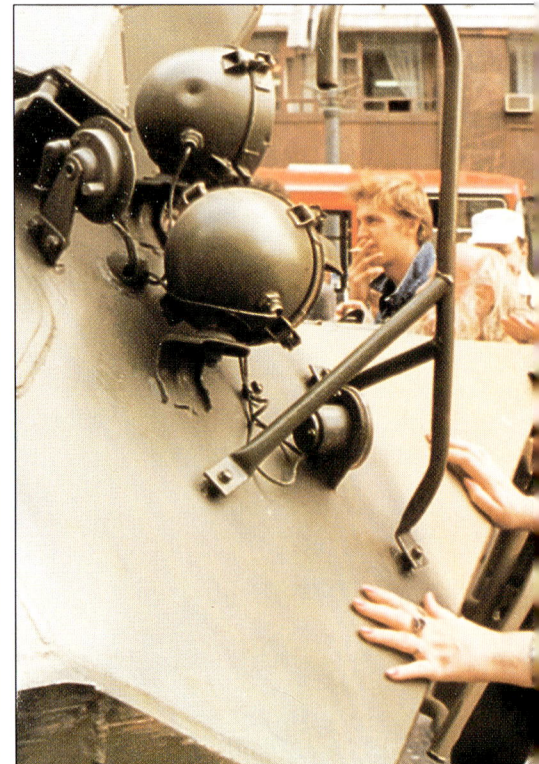

In June 1991 Boris Yeltsin was elected President of Russia.

IT WAS NOT easy to turn vision into reality. In the first four years of perestroika the Soviet Union's economy got worse. There were shortages of consumer goods and food. Gorbachev and his advisers decided to develop a more democratic system of government.

In August 1991 Muscovites

> *"Russia's trouble was never a shortage or an abundance of reformers. The trouble was an inability to adhere to a consistent policy."*

In the same year communist countries in Eastern Europe took their independence, while Gorbachev and Shevardnadze received promises of economic aid from the new US President, George Bush.

Within the USSR, many of the republics demanded freedom. The Baltic states wanted independence, Georgian uprisings were suppressed and there was fighting in Armenia, Azerbaijan and Moldova.

Meanwhile, in Moscow, President Gorbachev lost many of his political friends and allies.

Boris Yeltsin led popular resistance in Moscow in August 1991.

resisted the Soviet army.

Gorbachev thought that with the KGB and army on his side he could still make his reforms. Elections in the republics in 1990 introduced many nationalist politicians, and the 28th Communist Party Congress refused to follow his wishes. Frightened, he allowed Yeltsin to experiment with reforms.

In August 1991 Vice-President Yanayev, with the KGB, army and police, tried to seize power from Gorbachev. Yeltsin had the rebels imprisoned and used his victory to weaken Gorbachev's position further. On 24 August 1991, Gorbachev resigned as Communist Party general secretary.

The 'New' Russia

BORIS YELTSIN started his political career in Sverdlovsk, now known by its former name of Ekaterinburg, where he was very popular. Gorbachev called him to Moscow in 1985, and made him Moscow City leader and a member of the ruling committee, known as the politburo. Two years later Yeltsin criticised the way perestroika was being introduced, and was dismissed from his posts. He had his revenge in March 1989, when he was elected as a people's deputy despite Communist Party opposition. He travelled extensively abroad and in the USA, and won many elections within the country. By 1991 he was the democratically elected President of Russia.

IN NOVEMBER 1991 the Communist Party of the Soviet Union was banned. In December of the same year, Yeltsin signed an agreement with the elected leaders of the republics of Ukraine and Belarus, which set up the Commonwealth of Independent States (CIS).

The forming of the Commonwealth of Independent States, 1991.

Yeltsin invited other states to join the CIS. The Baltic states were already independent and refused. Georgia and Azerbaijan were reluctant for a while, but eventually they joined the Commonwealth.

Yeltsin's new Russia inherited many problems – a difficult economy, enormous social deprivation and rising crime.

It was important that he should introduce reforms as quickly as possible.

Yegor Gaidar became First Deputy Prime Minister and launched new economic policies with another reformer, Genadii Burbulis. Their main aim was the privatisation of industry and agriculture, to boost the economy.

Is Democracy Working?

Tensions remain, despite reforms

AFTER 1992 the new Russian democracy was very fragile. There were enormous price rises, and 12 million people were unemployed. The West gave emergency aid and gradually shops were filled with goods, although the queues are still slow to disappear.

In 1993 the old parliament refused to dissolve itself, and Yeltsin sent in troops to force the members out of its building, the White House in Moscow. The 1993 elections later voted an anti-Yeltsin majority into the Federal Assembly (parliament).

However, the new constitution (laws) meant that the Federal Assembly could not oppose the President, so Yeltsin retained his position. Yeltsin's power in the parliament is therefore very shaky. As a result, Russian democracy remains fragile.

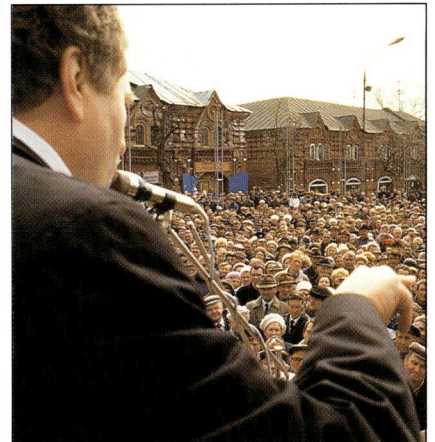

Vladimir Zhirinovsky.

Nationalism Grows

Vladimir Zhirinovsky, an extreme Russian nationalist whose policy is based on the hatred of non-Russians, is becoming very popular. In the 1991 presidential election, he attracted several million votes and his party, the Liberal Democrats, gained a quarter of the vote (78 seats) in the Russian parliament. Since 1991, especially when he is abroad, he has made many racist statements. He blames other countries and peoples for all Russia's problems, and plans to make the country the most powerful in the world.

Yeltsin attacked the old parliament with troops in 1993.

War at Home

IN 1991 General Dzhokhar Dudayev, the President of Chechenya (Chechnya in Russian), declared the independence of the tiny republic. For three years Yeltsin did nothing. But in December 1994, Russia invaded.

The Chechen soldiers have only basic, old-fashioned equipment. Most of the Russians are young recruits, with little or no experience of war.

The Chechen fighters delayed the Russian advance into their capital, Grozny, for a few weeks. But despite their efforts, the Russians have tried to bomb and shell the republic, in the southwestern part of Russia, into submission. Inexperienced Russian pilots have bombed flats and civilian areas, rather than their intended targets such as the Presidential Palace, the television tower and military bases. Many people have been forced to leave their homes. The devastating bombardments by the Russians have turned Grozny, once a busy, important city, into little more than a ghost town where people are afraid to live. The exact number of casualties in the war is unknown, but both sides have suffered heavy losses.

For the first time, the Russian people have been able to watch their troops fighting on television, and have seen the destruction caused to Chechenya and the hardships inflicted on its people. Many Russians think that the war is a mistake and that it will drag on for years, with neither side being able to win.

US-Russian cooperation in space funded a joint mission in 1994.

Forging a New Partnership

AFTER YEARS of economic troubles, Russia needs help from the West to achieve stability.

Years of isolation from the West and lack of experience in the successful management of factories and agriculture mean that Russia needs practical advice from Western experts and technicians, as well as a great deal of financial aid.

The Prime Minister, Chernomyrdin, has eliminated most of what he calls 'romantic reformers', and is aiming for concrete economic reforms.

He has obtained $28 billion from the Group of Seven industrialised countries and several loans from the International Monetary Fund (IMF).

However, Western countries are not investing as much as Russia would like them to, as they fear further political upheavals. If Zhirinovsky were to win the presidential election in 1996, there is a danger that democracy would collapse.

Into Space

The most promising area of joint initiatives is in space. The USA is cooperating with Russia on future missions on the Mir space station. Since its launch in 1986, Mir has been occupied continually by a series of crews from the USA and USSR. The cosmonauts spend their time carrying out experiments and making observations of the Earth.

Astronauts from France and Germany are being trained in Russia and are flying in space on board other Russian spacecraft. There will also be future cooperation with Russia in aeronautics and in exploration for oil and gas.

A Mir cosmonaut on his return to Earth in 1994.

Who Pays for the Clean-Up?

The legacy of industrialisation

The disposal of nuclear weapons will be a long, difficult task.

THE NUCLEAR industries harmed the USSR to a much greater extent than the rest of the world. Two nuclear accidents devastated the Urals, and nuclear testing damaged large areas of Kazakhstan.

The European Union has promised to finance the clean-up of the Chernobyl accident and the building of a new power station. The USA is paying for the destruction of Russian missiles and the conversion of Russian warheads into fuel for chemical weapons and peaceful nuclear uses. Ukraine will get $300 million in US aid to dismantle its long-range missiles and warheads. Some Russian politicians are opposed to this, saying that Russia does not want to be alone without such weapons. The military and industries do not want to end nuclear production, as exports are still flourishing and are paid for in US dollars.

People Take to the Streets

People in Russia are not used to demonstrating and protesting. Under communism, only a few brave human rights activists took part in demonstrations, and most of them suffered severely for their actions, at the hands of the secret police. Nowadays, however, people are free to demonstrate, and there are frequent protests against nuclear weapons (right) and the influence of the Mafia.

Better Relations?

Yeltsin meets Western leaders

A T THE MOMENT, the new, fragile democracy in Russia seems to depend on the political survival of President Yeltsin. Recently, however, Yeltsin has been suffering from bad health. If he were forced to retire, this could have a dramatic effect on the presidential election in 1996, and could lose the support of many other countries for Russia.

Yeltsin met US President Bill Clinton in 1994.

Western countries are opposed to all Yeltsin's rivals, especially Zhirinovsky. Yeltsin has recently met US President Bill Clinton and other Western leaders, spreading the view that if he falls, Russian democracy might be in danger.

Such fears have been increased by a recent statement from the foreign minister, Andrei Kozyrev, that Russia would use force to protect Russians living in nearby states. Russia has also agreed to sell a nuclear reactor to Iran.

Troops returning from Eastern Europe face a difficult future.

The Army Returns

Now that the powers of the KGB and special police have been reduced, Yeltsin needs the army's support. The army is in crisis, and has to cut its spending drastically. Soldiers returning from former communist countries need jobs. Yeltsin's relations with the army have been strained by scandals about Mafia arms deals. The returning soldiers have been received with hostility in Russia. Yeltsin had hoped for victory in the Chechen war, to strengthen his position and boost low troop morale, but this is unlikely.

The Future for Russia

In Russia there is still a strong, pro-communist minority which holds regular street demonstrations (right). However, a return to communism seems unlikely, even though the communist parties have 119 seats in parliament. The longer democracy survives, and the more the economy strengthens, the less likely such a return becomes. Russia could greatly improve its economic development, given a supportive political situation both at home and abroad.

CHRONOLOGY

6th-8th centuries AD Slavic tribes emigrate to Russia
c. 882 Prince Oleg unites city states Kiev and Novgorod
987 Vladimir converts to Christianity
1206 Gengis Khan launches conquest of world
1240 Batu Khan ruins Kiev
1462-1505 Ivan III conquers Russian city states
1533-84 Ivan IV ('the Terrible') conquers Kazan Tatars
1613 Election of Mikhail Romanov to throne
1682-1725 Peter I ('the Great') modernises Russia
1761-96 Catherine II ('the Great') updates Russia
1801-25 Alexander I joins Napoleonic wars
1825-55 Nicholas I tries to freeze Russia's development

1855-81 Alexander II makes reforms, but is assassinated
1881-94 Alexander III turns Russia into police state.
1894-1917 Nicholas II is weak and ineffective
1905 First popular revolution
1914 First World War
1917 Feb/Mar: first revolution; Nicholas abdicates Oct/Nov: Bolsheviks led by Lenin seize power
1918-1920 Civil war
1922 Creation of USSR
1924 Death of Lenin; Stalin bids for power
1936 Great Purge is launched
1939 Nazi-Soviet pact starts Second World War
1941 Great Patriotic War
1945 Soviet armies occupy Eastern Europe
1947 Start of cold war

1953 Death of Stalin
1956 Eastern Europe rises against communism
1957 Khrushchev becomes leader after denouncing Stalin
1962 Cuban missile crisis; start of nuclear 'arms race'
1964 Khrushchev dismissed; replaced by Brezhnev
1968 Czechoslovakia rebels; occupied by Soviet armies
1972 Arms control treaties by Brezhnev and Nixon
1982 Brezhnev dies
1985 Gorbachev becomes leader; launches perestroika
1989 Eastern Europe deposes communist leaders
1991 Boris Yeltsin becomes President; CIS Agreement
1993 US-USSR treaty; White House stormed; free elections
1994 Invasion of Chechenya

Photocredits
Abbreviations: t-top, m-middle, b-bottom, r-right, l-left
All the pictures in this book were supplied by Frank Spooner Pictures, apart from the following pages: Cover,
4t, 5t & b, 8b, 9t, 10l, 14, 15, 16, 17, 18, 19, 20t & b, 21b, 23m, 24, 26t & b, 27t: Novosti Picture Library;
10: The Mansell Collection; 12, 13: Mary Evans Picture Library; 21t & m: Rex Features.

Herald INTERNATIONAL Tribu

PUBLISHED WITH THE NEW YORK TIMES AND THE WASHINGTON POST

have been too
claim immunity
ments that do not
aplications for

Mr Clarke has admitted
signing six public interest
immunity certificates
during his year at the
Home Office on security
grounds.

London, Thursday, April 13, 1995

Clin
Is N
De

Α ΚΑΙ ΘΑ ΣΥΓΚΑΛΕΣΕ

ΩΝ Π
EYP

Σήμερα: Συνέρχ
Γαλανός: Συνάν

Γράφει Α. Λυκαυγης

ΤΙΣ σοβαρές του ανησυχιι
εξελίξεις κι ενδεχόμεν
ρότεσς της Δημοκρατίας
ιουβούλιο την
νενέσθ

oys
fiat
to
Talks

Overture
solve Issue
ian Security

lan Cowell

'Cleansers' of Muslims Show No Sign of Yielding

By Roger Cohen
New York Times Service

ZVORNIK, Bosnia-Herzegovina — Up through a ghostly terrain of smashed and ransacked former Muslim homes, Branko Grujic led the way, intent on showing off his crowning contribution to what he calls the victory of Serbian Orthodox Christianity over Islam in Bosnia.

Mr Grujic, the mayor of this northeastern Bosnian town now controlled by Serbs and completely "cleansed" of its 40,000 prewar Muslim inhabitants, has a pet project. It stands atop the escarpment that overlooks Zvornik and the meandering sweep of the Drina River.

Arriving at the summit of the cliff, Mr Grujic paused to kiss a wooden cross he has had erected before declaring: "The Turks destroyed the Serbian church that was here when they arrived in Zvornik in 1463. Now we are rebuilding the church and reclaiming this as Serbian land forever and

There is indeed a cruel finality to

of thousands of Muslims have been pushed out by force, many of them to Bosnian government-controlled territory around Srebrenica and Tuzla.

Such activity, and the uncompromising attitude of Mr Grujic, suggest that Serbian readiness to accept new peace proposals from the United States may be scant

Serbs in general remain committed to holding onto land they have seized by force and

The UN deploys troops around T
in preparation for an aid

appear to have hap
Bosnian politic
with Mus

"Look
pon
shi

Le gouvernement israélien divisé
face aux colons extrémistes

Les tractations continuent en Israël à pro-
opposé les membres du gouvernem
l'entrée au gouvernement du parti
droite Tsomet du général Rafaël
souhaitée par M. Rabin,
de gauche Meretz, qui
doxe Shass, qui

mesures à prendre contre les
veille, entre 25 000 et 30
dont quelques milliers
à Tel-Aviv pour réc
diate des extrémi
occupés, voire, p
des colons

EL

PRECIO: 100 PTS.

PIDEN «DEMOCRACIA PA

tias europe
de m